CENIZAS

CENIZAS

Poems

CYNTHIA GUARDADO

THE UNIVERSITY OF
ARIZONA PRESS
TUCSON

The University of Arizona Press
www.uapress.arizona.edu

We respectfully acknowledge the University of Arizona is on the land and territories of Indigenous peoples. Today, Arizona is home to twenty-two federally recognized tribes, with Tucson being home to the O'odham and the Yaqui. Committed to diversity and inclusion, the University strives to build sustainable relationships with sovereign Native Nations and Indigenous communities through education offerings, partnerships, and community service.

ISBN-13: 978-0-8165-4617-6 (paperback)
ISBN-13: 978-0-8165-4618-3 (ebook)

Cover design by Leigh McDonald
Cover art by Leslie Guardado
Designed and typeset by Leigh McDonald in Bell MT Std 10.25/14 and Good Headline Pro (display)

Publication of this book is made possible in part by the proceeds of a permanent endowment created with the assistance of a Challenge Grant from the National Endowment for the Humanities, a federal agency.

Library of Congress Cataloging-in-Publication Data
Names: Guardado, Cynthia, 1984– author.
Title: Cenizas : poems / Cynthia Guardado.
Other titles: Camino del sol.
Description: Tucson : University of Arizona Press, 2022. | Series: Camino del sol: a Latinx literary series
Identifiers: LCCN 2021061634 (print) | LCCN 2021061635 (ebook) | ISBN 9780816546176 (paperback) | ISBN 9780816546183 (ebook)
Subjects: LCSH: Immigrants—El Salvador—Poetry. | Salvadorans—United States—Poetry. | El Salvador—History—Civil War, 1979–1992—Refugees—Poetry. | LCGFT: Poetry.
Classification: LCC PS3607.U2326 C46 2022 (print) | LCC PS3607.U2326 (ebook) | DDC 811/.6—dc23/eng/20220118
LC record available at https://lccn.loc.gov/2021061634
LC ebook record available at https://lccn.loc.gov/2021061635

Printed in the United States of America
♾This paper meets the requirements of ANSI/NISO Z39.48-1992 (Permanence of Paper).

an immigrant is a person between nations, an elevator between floors

—GUILLERMO GÓMEZ-PEÑA

CONTENTS

FOREWORD

THE INHERITED PAST is bittersweet because along with the histories, memories, and stories, pain and trauma are also passed down from one generation to the next. The saving grace is that strength, too, derives from the people who came before. In *Cenizas*, the Salvadoran Civil War (1979–1992) continues to haunt the speaker, who is now experiencing the pangs of losing those beloved family members who had survived their homeland's most embattled period. Yet it's the perseverance of the dead that breathes life into the bereaved:

> all the blood inside my body
> is a stream tethered to the roots of trees
> stretching thousands of years
> they have carried me for generations
> from the past into my physical body (the future)
>
> .   .   .   .
>
> my soul bloomed in the dark of Abuela's house
> & migrated to another country
> where my ancestors prayed for my parents
> prayed over my unborn body
> until my DNA was full of thunderstorms
> until the day of my return

Salvadoreños have become the sixth largest immigrant group in the United States. This community grew exponentially from 94,000 to 465,000 between 1980 and 1990, most of them refugees fleeing the civil war. By 2008, the year they were eligible to register for Temporary Protected Status, that number had grown to 1.1 million. The current estimate is 2.3 million. Cynthia Guardado's poems don't focus on statistics, but they do press on the pulse of this exodus from El Salvador, which looms large over the people and places that inhabit her work. "All my people have been born from the ashes of vol-canoes," she writes, invoking an ancestral lineage that has been witnessed by the twenty active volcanoes of El Salvador, but also one that has endured the travesty of violence committed against Salvadoreños. The ashes—cenizas in the title—are the aftermath of turbulence, natural and human made.

One of the privileged insights that *Cenizas* offers its readers is the lived experience of a child of immigrants who returns repeatedly to the homeland. El Salvador keeps pulling the speaker back, and despite warnings of danger, she still manages to find beauty among the ruins:

> Everyone says I should be afraid of you
> as if you have never held me in your hands.
> You have offered me what I cannot find anywhere else—
> the way rain falls on tin roofs & mud sticks to our feet.

And when the speaker visits her family's hometown of Chalatenango, she arrives eager to connect, to find her place in the world her family left behind. When she's asked to help make pupusas, however, she understands she is being perceived as too far removed from her cultural heritage: "They wonder if I am really / a Chalateca like them." Nonetheless, she claims her birthright. The sacrifices of her ancestors are too precious and too mean-ingful to become brittle and break:

> Everyone says I should be afraid of you,
> but all I want to do is return to you—
> to run my hands through the humidity,
> to let the fireflies call me tenderly into night,
> to let you kiss me with ashes on your tongue.

Cenizas offers an arresting portrait of a family whose fate was shaped by global politics and conflict. It sets out to reimagine a country that has been defiled by the actions of those who sought power. But most importantly, it insists on bringing both family and country to a place close to wholeness, by reinforcing the love bond between them.

—*Rigoberto González*

ACKNOWLEDGMENTS

I AM DEEPLY grateful to all of the editors of the following journals and anthologies where these poems, sometimes in different form, first appeared:

Palabra: A Magazine of Chicano & Latino Literary Art: "An Old Indio's Tango"
    (now titled "Papá Víctor: Folklore")

The Acentos Review: "Emptying Your Apartment the Day After Christmas"
    (now titled "Before We Send My Cousin's Body Back to El Salvador")

The Packinghouse Review: "Eating in the Middle of the Night" (now titled
    "Los Estados Is How I Forget")

Huizache: The Magazine of Latino Literature: "Terrorist Attack by the Mara
    on a City Bus" (now titled "Mejicanos, San Salvador") and "Mosca"

The Journal of Latina Critical Feminism: "Your Tía Finds You un Taxi Seguro"

bozalta: "Potrero" and "A Morning en la Casa de Mi Abuelo"

The Wandering Song: Central American Writing in the United States: "Eight
    Women in a Kitchen y una Poeta"

Poetry Magazine: "In Exchange for My Absence" (now titled "Aislado")

CENIZAS

GUARDADO:

1. THE GUARDED 2. PUT AWAY

The rounded monosyllabic sounds
a ritual chant: *Gwarr-dah-doh*

Gwarr-dah-doh. A barrier builds
in the rolling *erre* harsh against

an English tongue. In El Salvador,
my name lifts out of the mouths

of herders, moves across the land.
My name a destination, Los Guardados,

a place of ancestors & colonization. This name—
branded on my family—rises out of

the ashes in the wind. I can trace each syllable
back to our cantón: Buena Vista. It runs thick

in my lineage: it is my mother's maiden name.
I am Guardado Guardado:

a name that hides history from itself.

THE HISTORIAN

for my mother

No hay bibliotecas en donde estamos guardados y la academia es mi mamá. I call her (on WhatsApp) to learn about our history while sitting (alone) in a town (Stourbridge, England) because still she is the only person I know who knows my history—knows that Abuelo era militar (in 1948). I'm looking for reasons to understand a lifetime of alcoholism, & she tells me, *Perdió su mamá cuando era niño.* I'm surprised & not (because trauma) that my great-grandmother (una india) died de un susto (fear in 1942) after a man threatened my great-grandfather (a white man) over money. I am writing this: because no one else has (& don't we deserve history too?). I'm tired of turning to a (disappearing) time line where the only highlights are the smell of a cantón & the ashes (of everyone) (before us). My mother (stands in the kitchen half a world away) tries to remember (for me) (for her); her research is in the deep sea (of memory), & before we hang up she tells me (twice), *If I find out anything else, I'll let you know. If I find out anything else, I'll let you know.* When the call is over, I write (porque yo también soy la academia) this poem instead of writing the poem about Abuelo's trauma (because I don't need to prove to you why we are important).

ARS POETICA

Why didn't Mamá Chila leave Abuelo?
Did she look for him when he disappeared for weeks at a time?

My mother's breath tunnels through the receiver,
& in the air between us
her words attempt to restore order.
She says, *Your abuela was respectable. She was devout.*

I ask, *Why did you leave?*
but she does not answer me; instead she asks,
Where could she have gone with all of us?
My mother sighs. *What are you looking for?*

I say, *There is so much I want to know.*
I feel as if you are the only one with answers.

———

       i cannot explain to her
       how each night i see all of our ghosts
       how our ancestors hide in the planes
       how they call me back to find the truth
       in the cenizas of the alcaldía
       in an unwritten village in a country mythical
       across distance like our history erased & buried
       i cannot explain to her how i hear tongues
       click in the early morning

they rapidly whisper in Nawat
the answers to the questions
i ask from this universe

———

My mother waits for me to say more, to fill
the silence that lingers. But here the wind devours
our words, the ones we cannot bear—
each syllable fills the stretched mouth
of the sky until nothing else can be said.
I'll call you tomorrow, Má.

SIX MONTHS BEFORE ABUELA'S DEATH

I guide Mamá Chila north as we walk on Inglewood Avenue
to St. John's Church; a black man in white
outside the fried fish market is covered in remnants
of flesh & batter. I'm only eleven years old,
but today my mother has asked me to lead.
I nervously search for the steeple to emerge
behind City Hall & point to a distant mirage.
This is the first time Mamá Chila visits los Estados,
& she tells me that villagers used to walk on their knees
during Semana Santa en el cantón. For three days
they offered their bodies. When we arrive, the sacristía
is filled with rows of women praying.
Abuela instructs me to kneel, my sweaty knees sticking
to the tattered vinyl. Instead of closing my eyes,
I watch the mantillas fall onto the shoulders of women,
their grief unfolding in the swirls of draping lace.
Who has taught them to bow their heads this way, to avert eyes,
to pray through pursed lips? Whispers drip from the ceiling,
& I watch the sheer fabric pull with every nod.
I pretend to pray, but when I bow my head
I see the hem of Mamá Chila's knee-length skirt rise
to reveal scars: jagged layers of skin like
the folds of clasped hands; & in this moment
I wonder why her prayers have gone unanswered.
I hear Mamá Chila's quiet words, & again
she asks God to heal Abuelo. I lean closer to her
but only hear a *shhhhh* escape from her pursed lips
to quiet the questions she knows I will not ask.
She reaches for my hand. *Oremos*, she says.

PAPÁ VÍCTOR: FOLKLORE

El Indio's mistress dances in the aroma of roasted agave. Her bottle-shaped hips follow the rhythm of ritual. Together they extract the piña, cook it in hot rocks, crush it, leave it to ferment.

Day after day his wife grinds maize to feed their nine children: three sons named Víctor, three daughters, & three more. He thinks the children are stories he's heard from people he knows. A villager stands in the dirt road outside of el Indio's fábrica calling with news that his wife has collapsed, fallen into a coma, & died.

El Indio's three youngest children—feeling bereaved—visit him. Divided by a wire fence they stare, unsure of their father, his eyes empty as hollow wood. Too incoherent to find the key, he hooks his fingers through the barrier between them, tries to remember which three they are.

His skin hard as clay stretches over his swollen body. He stands in his underwear baring a crooked smile. He is alone now. His wrinkles like growth rings in the pockets of his face gather each time he loses a child—each time they choose to leave him behind. He stares into a mirror far back into the cavernous rooms of his mind. Sees himself in an empty field once a forest, the lone tree among the ashes.

CALL ME REFUGEE I

The bomber plane moves north, away from the smell of flesh;
smoke pulses each time the helicopter's blade cuts air. A young pilot
grips the controls; he isn't prepared to bomb another village. Below
a little girl carries her youngest brother, & no one sees her feet sift

the smoke; it pulses. Every time the helicopter's blade cuts air, a young man
searches for his family, prays his eldest daughter isn't already gone. She is
a little girl carrying her youngest brother, but no one sees her. Feet sift
mud, & he's afraid all his children will be slaughtered. Death

searches for his family. His eldest daughter is already gone; she was only
a child when she watched her villagers herded like animals
in mud. The pilot's afraid now; all his children have been slaughtered. Death
engulfs villages, like a tsunami. When another missile drops a woman hides

a child. She watches her villagers be herded like animals
in cages, rounded up & shot by soldiers; she bears witness. Fire
engulfs villages like a tsunami. After another missile drops, a woman hides,
& she prays for the young pilot: *Our Father, who art in heaven, free us from*

these cages. Soldiers shoot rounds, & she bears witness to fire.
He grips the controls; he isn't prepared to bomb another village. Below
she prays for the young pilot: *Our Father, who art in heaven, free us from these*
bomber planes. Move them north, away from the smell of our flesh.

REFLEJO

Untitled (Niños I), San Antonio Los Ranchos, Chalatenango, El Salvador, 1988, by U.S. photographer Donna DeCesare

I.

a boy plays with the carcass of a bomb,
its broken container the aftermath

from attacks on his village. the placard says 1988;
he is the same age as me when i board planes

in & out of war. in the photo his furrowed brow
weighs heavily like the ghost of his mother in the rubble

of buildings still crumbling. at age four,
i was convinced the only force against me

was a preschool fence: the red taillights
of my father's car disappearing. somehow

i've forgotten the war that wages in Chalate—
the sound of bullets muffled by pouring rain

& two kinds of thunder. in this photo the boy
poses alone, lifts his arm higher as if to show me

the bomb's fractured tail, its metal edges
like teeth. i imagine his parents must be just outside

the frame when a white woman takes his picture.
But this photo will not tell us: his mother was killed

by militares & his father joined la guerrilla;
instead i watch the boy glide his finger—

small like mine—over the sharpness of steel,
peer into the open belly of the bomb.

II.

querido Abelito,

hay distancias que no podemos sobrepasar
como los fantasmas que nos ven

entre las hojas del aguacate moviéndose
frenéticamente —queriendo tocarnos—

debajo de la lluvia de estrellas muertas.
nunca nos conoceremos en los cuarenta kilómetros

de tu casa a la de mi abuela en Buena Vista
donde me da miedo dormir. en ese tiempo

no entendía cómo se quemaban
los montes, ni cómo a un lado de tu casa

caían bombas. nunca nos conoceremos cuando
me regrese a Los Ángeles —4639 kilómetros

fuera de tu hogar. hay distancias que son inmensas
e invisibles como los volcanes debajo de las montañas

de Chalate. a los cuatro años nosotros no sabemos

qué nos va pasar en la vida (o, cuando yo escriba de ti,

si todavía tú vivirás o si habrás encontrado un refugio
eterno en alguna esquina del universo).

III.

at ten years old, caution tape wrapped around
a building in Inglewood like a noose still waiting,

& i imagine a dead body (even if i've
never seen one) (or at least this is what i believe).

drifting among us is the spirit of the dead boy;
he lifts his finger to touch mine from an alternate

universe as i point at the bullet holes in concrete
& plaster. at ten years old, Abelito sits on a hill—

a volcano brewing beneath—& hopes his father
will return from la guerrilla (i read this in a book

at thirty-six years old, & it is the first time i know his name).
at ten years old, Abelito & i hold in our hands a reality—

stretching across space—hoping to repair the burn
of bombs & bullets, the way only children can dream of.

i know i don't remember much of my childhood
(& now my fading memories try to make their way

into this poem i've been writing for a decade);

the black hole that sits in my brain swallows up years,

& maybe this is my body's way of protecting me,
the way the shell of a tortoise resists certain kinds of death.

PARALLEL UNIVERSE

after a five-hour flight from El Salvador to Los Angeles

In the dark of my mother's room
a portal opens into my abuela's house in Buena Vista:

tall ceilings, revealed beams, bats hanging in the shadows,
& another sleepless me afraid of night. I lie

next to my mother, my nails digging into the back of her
nightgown (afraid she will disappear like Abuela

into the portal's open mouth). After weeks en el cantón
we have traveled back in time to los Estados

(where no one we love exists). I'm nine years old,
& the world has split in two. In the portal's eye I can still see

Abuela's body shrinking in the distance on an endless road.
I hear the wind howl against the veranda of her house,

electricity trembling in the storm. The portal
in my mother's room flickers a message—Morse code between

spaces, across the wreckage of time—telling us to teleport
back to the only place we call home. The day we left

the dog chased our lingering scent for miles;
Tío's truck kicked up dirt, & still the dog chased us

through the clouds. He ran faster & faster, like he knew
we weren't coming back. I believed he would leap onto

the back of the truck bed, his teeth clinging to my clothes,
like a plea for us to listen, to stay, to not leave them behind.

MY FATHER'S TESTIMONY AT ST. VINCENT DE PAUL, 1999

At fourteen, I sit alone in a back pew near the exit
while my father takes his turn at the altar.
I remove my headphones when his voice
begins to fill the golden dome of the church.
He tells a story about when I was nine,
the one in which he sent me to the toilet (punished
for having wet myself). His voice echoes in the dome
when he says how he hit me across the mouth.
I remember my nose bled into my hands
& my older sister watched in fear.
My father skips ahead to when he left
for his usual graveyard shift,
& here he remaps our history with a part
of the story I had only learned to long for.
He admits he cried when he was alone,
felt guilty for his inability to show his daughters
he was not a monster. I cry quietly
as my father shares with a room
full of strangers what he could never tell me:
he confesses how he wishes in his youth
he'd been tender like his words are now.

HOW I REMEMBER IT, AFTER HE HIT ME

An exposed nail punctures
my thigh when my father hits me
with a piece of wood—
at eleven I am forgiving.

I can only force small words out
of the tightness in my throat:

> *Look what you did.*

That was the last time he hit me
(or at least this is what I believe).
(Is this the story
I retell—the one in which
I recall my father's shame?)

My father is intentional in the way
he doesn't hit my youngest sister,
the way Abuela taught him, too.

Abuela stood over him without restraint:
switch in hand
her arm pulling back
until everything was blurry.

He is intentional now
because the switch,

the nearby tree,
the piece of wood
are all connected in memory.
(My father told me this, right?)

I can't find the moment in which
he shared this truth, but I do
just barely see a memory of Abuela—

her shaking body menacing
& swaying with violence.

My father will learn
how to love her even harder
in her old age.
He will be forgiving
when he holds her small hand against his,
imagines this was how
she cradled his small body after birth.

.

CALL ME REFUGEE II

in the middle of the country, i slip away from my mother, get lost in the booming sound of bombs. militares carry rifles; i run into fields, find the old train tracks curving out of the mountain's mouth. if i follow them they will lead me home. in the distance animals rest on the rails. i get closer, see they are the bodies of three boys only a little older than me. they lie one on top of the other, their faces tender like maíz morado. i grab a stick—a little frightened—begin to inspect them. has a bomb torn off a limb? have bullets ripped through them? their blood is dry, absorbed into the earth, the dirt darker now. the sun is hot when i find my way back to el cantón. i tell everyone what i have witnessed. i say, *if you want i can take you there.*

THERE ISN'T ENOUGH MONEY FOR YOUR GRIEF

when you answer the phone
the line crackles over the distance
a voice   you barely recognize
calls from El Salvador to say
               Mamá Chila ha muerto

you are
only a teenager

your mom can't afford   to take you
the line dangles
as she packs a suitcase

she will carry   the weight of grief

you wish you could climb inside

live in the darkness
of a journey   to another country

on the red-eye
your mother will wish
          she had listened
a few days ago   a voice warned
her mother had been sent to
               el hospital de Chalate

you remember your aunt crying
over her dead brother
she told you
la gente sólo llega al hospital a morir

you think
no one ever returns whole

you don't get to attend the burial
this   another burden   you   carry
because your feet walk   in both worlds

you'll learn
your tío
sin papeles   will not return
will not say goodbye
as your mother
will do

years later your mother will tell you
she dressed Abuela
for the funeral
applied makeup onto
her mother's cold flesh

you'll know then
you'll never know   a goodbye   that   intimate

porque
en los Estados Unidos

las distancias   se multiplican
como los muros   de las fronteras

BEFORE WE SEND MY COUSIN'S BODY BACK TO EL SALVADOR

in memory of Doris Salguero

I kneel in front
of your open refrigerator
the day after Christmas.
I am emptying your apartment.
I reach for wilted lettuce like prayer;
when I lower it into a trash bag
its withering leaves break against my skin.

I believe if I am careful
this will feel like less of a waste.

Your gallon of milk pushes against
three-week-old quesadillas
from El Salvador—the foil
still bears your mother's handwriting.

I whisper little prayers,
bless food you thought
you'd have time to eat.

I believed you'd be safe here
but now mold extends onto everything.
There is nothing left

except for the refrigerator's light
reflecting upon its own emptiness.
I carry this bag of fragments into the garage,
linger in the concrete chill.

A few days later I will learn
you were murdered
right here:

      your blood pooling,
      your blood wiped clean.

The only evidence: your shadow
pressing into this soiled ground.

LOS ESTADOS IS HOW I FORGET

I smell the clay oven in Abuela's house &
watch her prepare dinner,
chasing gallinas in the open kitchen.
Trees peek in when Abuela's hand curls perfectly
around the hen's throat. She whirls it—
the winning ticket in lotería—
until its neck splits in two.
She ties the hen's feet with care,
hangs it from a hook on the wall.

———

En los Estados nuestro cantón is a fiction
in a photograph of Abuela frozen in the
in-between; her spirit drifts across
imaginary borders. I fumble through layers
of memory, & nothing feels familiar
in this place. I clench a rusty steel cross
from Abuela until my knuckles turn white—
until I see the cows grazing in Buena Vista;
I smell the remnants of a storm & anxiously hold
the dampness of home. The distance fills me
with fear that this place is how I will forget.

———

Sleepless hunger lingers in the dark aisles
of a Greyhound from Fresno to Los Angeles.
A woman sits next to me, & somehow I know
this is Abuela. She tells me she is going
to Yuma as she rustles with the bag at her feet;
she says, *Me llamo Gloria*, offering a hard-boiled egg.
We eat through the darkness, pause
between bites to trickle chile onto yolks.
We talk through the middle of the night,
& I don't feel so alone anymore
as we savor the yolks shrinking
like waning moons in the palms of our hands.

LOS ESTADOS IS HOW I FORGET AGAIN

Your voice is lost in the faded film: your frozen frame,
hand on hip. You stare into boiling water, wait

for it to rise like I wait for your name
to surface from beneath my English words. I've forgotten

again how to call for you. En los Estados,
nadie te conoce. & I am afraid of time—

how it makes you disappear. I close my eyes, try to hear
the vowels that curl on my Salvadoran tongue. Slowly

the short *ch* sound comes to me. I am close to finding you,
& I hear the fragments

in my mind. When your name emerges from where
I've buried it I whisper it to myself like a chant of resurrection:

Maa maa Chee la
Maa maa Chee la
Maa maa Chee la

CALL ME REFUGEE III

Untitled (Dolor I), *Soyapango, San Salvador, El Salvador, 1989, by U.S. photographer Donna DeCesare*

The sound of grief resonates like the prolonged warning
of a muted trumpet. Villagers run & wave shards

of white cloth—flags frozen on black & white film. Their eyes
stay glued to the sky in prayer; they search for bomber planes

through clouds of ash. The woman who leads them refuses
to look back; her eyes darken as she stares into the road ahead.

Smoke rises from their burning homes, & a young girl
clings to the woman's arm; the girl's small jaw is caught open,

the deep crease of her mouth filled with a cry
no one will hear twenty years later. This museum, once a prison,

holds time still as the woman in the photo marks
Bible verses between her fingers. I lean my face

toward the glass, attempt to see the scriptures in her hand.
I watch the girl who stares directly into the camera

at the photographer who captures their retreat. In this moment,
they can think only of survival, & no one will imagine

themselves in an exhibit, next to a map of los Estados
that counts refugees (in the millions) who leave & leave.

WHAT MY NAME CARRIES

Luggage exits the belly of the plane,
& I collect what I've brought
from one country to another.

In Customs, I want to say, *Sí*
when the uniformed lady asks, *¿Salvadoreña?*
but she directs me behind two blonde

foreigners. To my left are the people
returning home—a single red belt
divides us. Those who've come back

wave navy-blue passports like flags;
their leather covers reveal a small outline
of a country (never fully mine).

On days like this I'm less certain where
I belong, my blood not enough
to prove I too am from here.

The immigration officer asks
if my parents were born
in El Salvador. He already has

the answer in a file, the baseline
of truth; I lie when he asks why
I came here. I don't tell him

I'm here to write about the war
or that I will travel to Perquín,
Morazán. He knows my last visit

was five years ago; he tells me this,
his voice high at the end like
a question I must answer. I lean into

the counter, remove the distance
between us, say, *Cómo pasa
el tiempo, ¿qué no?* He asks
where I will stay;
I tell him my tío is dying
& give him the address

of a priest—grief the only
language between us—
to explain why I've come here.

MEJICANOS, SAN SALVADOR

Passengers are showered in gasoline
by two young boys who threaten them
with AK-47s.* They scream
before a lit match is thrown.
The smell of gasoline terror.
I watch their arms break glass
as they try to squeeze their bodies out
of windows the size of oven doors.
Traffic has stopped, & all anyone can do
is watch them burn.
Later, when the bus lies charred
& caution tape sections off the city,
the smell of burning flesh will stick
in my hair, & I will be afraid
to wash it away, to let them go.

* On June 22, 2010, members of the Mara Salvatrucha gang attacked a city bus
in Mejicanos, San Salvador, burning fourteen people alive.

YOUR TÍA FINDS YOU UN TAXI SEGURO

San Salvador, El Salvador

My taxi driver don Pedro
waits for me outside la alcaldía
de Santa Tecla—
guards lean against walls,
rifles resting on hips.

>   *La gente siempre anda con precaución*
>   *—en la Capital es muy peligroso recoger gente*
>   *en la calle,* says don Pedro.

This district desolate,
except for the occasional
call of a voice, sits in darkness.
We drive away. The marketplace
sleeps—the energy of shuffling vendors
no longer lingers. A clap can be heard
releasing, & we try not to think of guns
as we listen to tarps snapping in the wind.

———

On our first drive together,
don Pedro squints his eyes—
crescent moons fixed
in the rearview mirror. He tells me

his wife is from Buena Vista,
the village of my childhood.

I ask his wife's name:
Lilia, he says.
& I know the *L*'s long *e*
the *lee lee aah*
taking root in my memory,
familiar to my tongue
like pickled radishes—
the color still changing.

Under the shadow of night
Metrocentro's
lights bloom like
ghosts rising in the dark.

———

Outside el hospital de Chalatenango,
don Pedro meets my parents.
We are caught in some kind of
odd union again:

strangers a few weeks ago,
& now he listens to us cry

over the groan of his engine.
We tell him my tío is dying.
He searches for gentle words
like we're friends he's known
for years. It rains hard,

& my sister, who is going
back to Los Angeles,
sobs in the back seat of his taxi.
The fifty kilometers ahead of us swell
like the distance between two countries.

DIASPORA

i. CREATION STORY: EL SALVADOR

In my mother's womb, in a universe of my own, every cell of her body held memory like DNA (now it is mine too.) Her heartbeats (our first song) are the chants of my mother's mother & our great-great-grandmothers. Before my physical body was fully formed, I saw my ancestors dance & hold hands in prayer as they told stories of homeland to summon me to the loma behind my great-great-great-grandmother's house.

ii. BIRTHPLACE: IN-BETWEEN

I've lived in a state of permanent limbo since my birth in Boyle Heights. I was born dying—I saw light rise out of my parents' bodies: their spirits lifting like the Seven Sisters, a cluster of bulbs stretching across the universe into Buena Vista.

In the hospital my blood was drawn over & over, the bottoms of my small feet dripping red; my mother said I was running out of veins & the doctors were running out of ideas.

In K-Town my mother held my fragile body in the sun, & after a while I was no longer dying (even if I was not fully here).

In me grew a deep silence (I would not speak); I had nothing to say (on earth, in this dimension). I could not utter words, my spirit silently clinging to the ashes of my ancestors—to the cells of my mother's womb.

III. REBIRTH: BUENA VISTA, EL SALVADOR

At almost two years old, I refused to utter words. I talked only to spirits in my dreams; they called us back like migrating birds who return to the same place thousands of miles away.

My father's body heard the call too; over the radio (in his red Fiat driving home from his graveyard shift) a man told him to take his daughters to Mamá Juana (my great-grandmother). My spirit knew her name even if I had never seen her in human form. My father had feared she would die before he could show her the future—his daughter's blooming.

IV. HOMELAND: WAR ZONE

My father was undocumented in 1986, & after many arguments with my mother (over the voice on the radio), we were flying. My mother refused to go into a war zone (undocumented) but she knew that she could not stop my father (undocumented) from flying home. She too had watched how (when he paced at night) small strands of white light extended across the distance, reaching for his body.

My father knew that in the grooves of his skin, in the weight of his cheek-bones, he carried a home invisible to the naked eye. It required a certain spirit (heavy with leaving) to see that he was not whole.

In 1986 the war was bodies piling in unmarked graves, los escuadrones de la muerte, militares raping girls, 500-pound bombs; was guerrilleros watching from the shadow of volcanoes; was my Tío Roberto living in exile in Mexico; was a constant state of fear for an entire people afraid to leave their homes (afraid to sleep in their beds).

& still, we went.

v. HOMELAND: MATRIARCH

My great-grandmother, Mamá Juana, held me the way she held my father's fragile body after birth. I climbed mango trees with cousins, & in me began to emerge words I would not speak en los Estados. I called out to my primas, *bichas bichas*, & right then the language my spirit always knew floated off the tip of my tongue—my mouth opened wide, my teeth tipping toward the sky.

vi. UNDOCUMENTED: REFUGEE

My mother fell ill while we were gone de un susto (from fear we wouldn't return from war, from fear my father would not be able to cross the border again). My father boarded a plane to Mexico with my sister & me. My aunt (the only documented person we knew) picked us up in Tijuana.

My father stayed behind, waited for the coyote he paid $500. The coyote was late. The coyote did not arrive on time. The coyote was not there. On our journey back, my father climbed a tree (it was not a mango tree) to hide from la migra. He waited for hours (or days) for the coyote, who was late.

When my aunt returned us to our mother (undocumented), her womb settled back into her body—her spirit bringing her back to life. & we waited (together) for my father (undocumented) to cross from the other side.

vii. MATRIARCH: DEATH

In late 1987, Mamá Juana died in Buena Vista. We did not go back undocumented.

In 1989, the four of us returned to El Salvador (documented), & at five years old I had waited what felt like my whole life to see Abuela again. Outside the airport, I searched the sea of people crowded together over the railing (that divided us). In the humidity, their damp arms clung to one another as they waited for those returning home. I searched (lost in their waving hands) for the face of Mamá Chila (this moment etched into my mind forever). She leaned over the railing, her green eyes searching for the face of her child. I saw Mamá Chila's shoulders rise as she waved a white handkerchief, & she was smiling, or maybe she was crying. This the first time my mother returned home (after almost dying in the desert) (after believing they would never see each other again).

IX. EL BUS: WELCOME HOME

On our trips to El Salvador my uncle picked us up en el bus. When we boarded el bus our grandmother, cousins, uncles, & aunts were like fire-flies in the night lighting our way on the three-hour trip home.

These are the bus rides I want to remember, the ones where we loaded our luggage & boxes of gifts—& hand-me-downs from my mom's bosses— into the pale blue back door del bus.

On the ride home, we twisted around in laughter as we stretched our bodies closer to one another. The sweaty dust in the air lifted around us, & all of our voices roared loudly over the engine.

In this reality, I don't remember a war, all my body holds is home.

x. BUS: MILITARES

We rode crowded buses from el tablón (near our cantón) to Sonsonate to visit Padre Héctor. In the humidity our clammy skin kissed strangers. Men hung out the back doors, the damp air a kind of relief. On the roof rattled the canastos filled with mangos, queso fresco, yuca y arroz.

I'm five years old the first time the militares stop us. Outside el bus our bodies line the road as they inspect documentos.

The silhouette of a man in the shadow of the sun stands on top of el bus. I watch him watch us as he inspects the canastos. In the corner of my eye are the armed militares working their way slowly down the line, in their hands a list of names (guerrilleros they've sentenced to death). They ask for cédulas, & my parents display their frayed paper cards.

One by one we are allowed to reboard el bus; we each shrink our bodies into safety when we pass the militar (whose face we cannot see) partially blocking the entry. When the bus pulls back onto the road, I sit in my father's arms staring out the window at the boy left behind (left for dead).

xi. PLANES: IN-BETWEEN

War erased the time line we were meant to be born with, & in it we emerged (refugees in the in-between).

We've boarded planes (over & over again), in & out of war. We are not whole here or there. We live in a constant state of shock; we hold our breath often, afraid we'll suddenly become extinct.

In the in-between is where Mamá Chila, Mamá Juana, & Mamá Olivia live; & Papá Chema, & Tío Roberto, & Tío Alejandro; & Doris. All my ancestors are in the El Salvador of my mind (the one I imagine while I sit on the beach in Los Angeles). There, they are never gone. They are in the home that lives in every cell of my body, a place far away (but more real than here).

All my people have been born from the ashes of volcanoes. All my people are buried en el panteón de San Rafael. Today we raked the fallen leaves off the tombs of our ancestors, & my mother said if she died in El Salvador to leave her there. I said, *Aquí vas a estar con todos* (in the in-between you'll exist forever).

CALL ME REFUGEE IV

the air fills with the smell of crated bananas
their odor escapes out of the darkness into our lungs
oxygen like a damp room evaporates & silently we pray
los Estados will be worth it while we stand with knees unbent
in this container behind padlocked doors our arms stiffly
stick to one another's as our bodies crowd together these crates
stacked like bricks seal us in shoulder to shoulder as we
hold our breath knowing it's been two whole days since the woman
beside us has died & so we take last breaths with her en el otro lado
we'll tell stories of how we survived & everyone will comment
on our weight loss & we'll pretend the whole thing was
a bad dream like the kind we'll say we've forgotten
even if it clings to the walls of our bedrooms when they go dark

TÍA GLORIA GETS HER BROTHER READY FOR THE WAKE

My brother is a sheet of ice in my hands when I elevate his legs one by one to slip on his dress socks. Three nights ago I wrapped a rosary around our fingers & we prayed Ave Marías in a hospital hallway. I knew then he would die. & still the touch of his cold flesh floods me like two years ago when my daughter came back from los Estados in a coffin filled with the dampness of death. At the edge of my brother's casket I lean close as if this is the last secret I will share with him— grief over what we've lost en el otro lado. I slowly tie his shoelaces like when he was just a boy & tell him, *I'm sorry I could not save you.* I fasten the loops, hold tightly, onto his stiff feet to keep him from falling.

MY FIRST FUNERAL EN EL CANTÓN, AGE TWENTY-SIX

the road is too narrow to fit cars passing
    (there is only one road
    to the dead)

the funeral home's truck plays loud music
a choir sings through a megaphone

around here tires kick up dirt
cover my tío's casket in a shroud of dust

we drive through clouds (floating like ashes)

pickup trucks full of villagers
    trail behind us   & I know
they've come to watch how we bury our dead

when we arrive at the graveyard
(where all the tombstones bear my name)

a little girl screams   & all our loss surfaces
like bodies in the desert

ODE TO AN ALCOHOLIC, AFTER DEPORTATION

my tío a dormant volcano lies on a gurney
in an upstairs hallway
his oxygen tank chained to a wall

a woman in starched white squeezes
a balloon-shaped pump   her grip
life support   tío's chest rises
when she forces air with her gloved hand

i lean close   clean his crusted lids
whisper to him
      climb to the top of Izalco when you're better

the nurse releases the pump
long enough to prove

he will survive this

tienen que tener fe she says
her hand closes into a fist
his lungs exhale & his wheeze
burrows into our ears

———

after he dies
my father & i prepare

the altar we cut the two-liter soda bottles
collected from villagers to make vases
for the wake   i decorate with aluminum foil
the ones my father has already sliced

on the other side of this wall
              lies my tío's body
mosquitoes   circle   above   us
in fluorescent light

spiders spin webs   their strands glow
like apparitions   i wonder if tío's spirit lingers here
reluctant to leave   my father
arranges flowers & i know
he has done this before
              a year ago un altar para su sobrina
              two years ago un altar para su madre

we pray until morning
a rosary around our fingers
this the last time
              tío will sleep   here

———

at the cemetery we wait together
& it will be here that we capture
a family photo   our bodies melting together
on this unmarked grave

it is hard to see where each of us begins
& i wonder if we've ever said
i love you like this
among what remains

the smell of dust rises
into our teeth & we are
captured   our contorted jaws
our attempt to consume this moment
in the background burial monuments bloom
  we shift our wrists & wave   our fingers
to brush off winter flies that cling

the gravedigger
will seal the burial chamber
stack each layer of brick slowly

& under the heat of the sun
our faces will reflect
off the top   of my tío's casket

they will   throw back the light

EL MURO: CARTA DE AMOR

I wish I could crumble
the concrete inside you
with my fingertips,

slide my hands
down your chest
& dislodge the thing

that holds love away
from us. I've tried everything:
sledgehammer, chainsaw.

I've run my fingers
gently across your
whole body hoping

somehow the love I carry
could enter—que de mi piel
salieran gotas de amor para
derrumbarte.
I don't have any metaphors

left to describe
how things always end;
I have to believe

(for my sanity)
the wall is as real as

this border between two
countries—the thing built
para no dejarnos entrar.

CALL ME REFUGEE V

for my mother

I slip my right foot into the plastic
mold of my brace. Adjust the straps over
my calf & ankle. I force my bound
foot into a shoe, this a reminder.
Polio haunts my right leg;
as a child each bare step
onto pebbled dirt roads was like pressing
into splintered wood. I wish I could
run when militares come to el cantón
to rape my primas, to rape mis vecinas.
When my body transforms—hips
widening, breasts erupting—
doctors' eyes grope me, examine the soft
muscles in my right thigh, & I pray
for los Estados to leave este dolor behind.

TWO YEARS AFTER HIS MOTHER'S MURDER

The flesh of deplumed hens toughens
in our hands—we're learning to package

death into plastic bags. On the line, hens
cackle, toss their feathers into frantic circles.

His abuelita shows me the tiny blade in her
palm & gestures for me to distract him.

She's afraid he'll remember his mother
is dead or that he'll eventually ask how

she was killed. Quietly, she slices the throat
of each hen while we talk of heat. Later, when

he asks what happened, Abuelita will protect him.
She'll say they're just sleeping. & he will

pretend to believe her, as if he could forget
about the hens he's already placed in bags,

their stiff faces pressed against plastic.

MOSCA

Flies swarmed around us. They crawled on our faces,
& we imagined somehow that they climbed inside our mouths.
We fought the moscas with bleach, thought it would purify us,
protect us from the buzzing & prickling in our ears.
My cousin asked if I wondered where they'd gone.
I realized then they had become absent in my mind;
the anxiety I'd felt earlier as I ate pacing in circles
had disappeared. He smiled & said, *Mira.*
His eyes pointed above our heads: hundreds of dormant flies
stuck to the metal roofing of the veranda. Motionless,
they seemed to rest as if what they craved
while the sun had shone was now left for tomorrow.
They followed the clock of the sky, & in this dusk the flies
retreated, not knowing if perhaps tomorrow they would die.

POTRERO

We scale up the hill through next year's
milpa, & the only things buzzing
are the flies. I imagine the sharp sound
of machinery & hear the squeal of a lever
echo from the fumigation tank my cousin
carries on his back. I am a tourist here;

I trail his soft footprints, mimic where
his steps fall, want to know how I
should tread. He sprays the harvest
& asks if I know who Karl Marx is.
The sweat on our backs is still, like the creek below,
a path drawn through the earth. He hauls

water on his shoulder in a cántaro,
its round belly pushing into
the base of his neck. We talk about imperialism.
He tells me his dreams: papaya fields & pinos
in rows on the curve of this loma.
I tell him at the root of everything

is colonialism. & he says: *Si tuviera que escoger los
Estados Unidos o El Salvador, yo viviera esta vida otra vez.*
I see a land mass float in the sky, ask
what it is, & my cousin laughs loudly, tells me
it's just a mountain peeking through the clouds.

EIGHT WOMEN IN A KITCHEN Y UNA POETA

San Salvador, El Salvador

The thump of palms on masa
resonates in the kitchen as two rabbits
cuddle in a corner close to the plancha's
heat. I am a guest here & sit at the table

with my notebook, pencil in hand—
draw rhythm with words: the curl
of the letter *c* like a bass clef hooking.
The women prepare pupusas next to me,

oil dissolves into air. They tell me
I write too much; I listen to the music
of their fingers flattening queso into masa,
making perfect circles. We are in our late

twenties, still trying to figure out where
we will go. They laugh loudly
like a choir when I say I will write
about them. I watch their expert hands,

& they ask if I can make pupusas;
I let them instruct me on what I haven't
done since childhood. How much masa
is too much? When I clap I must rotate

my palms, they say, move my fingers
away from each other like wings.
They wonder if I am really
a Chalateca like them. I lift the pupusa

I've made like a symbol—a grand
finale—place it on la plancha, hear it
sizzle. Together we watch the masa smoke
as if it too will ascend with time.

CALL ME REFUGEE VI

when we think of torture
the news tells us it's
Afghans   the Taliban
(but we know
it is los Estados)
now it's ISIS, they say

we've seen footage of hooded men
their hands & feet bound
tightly   behind them

        el capucho es
        una oscuridad
        eterna
        como la humedad
        de un cantón

these
torture displays
replay (1980)

decades apart

half   way

across   the   world

the only explanation
los   Estados   &
the   CIA   agent who

teaches military men torture

instructs others how to
nearly drown someone
how to   not   but just
barely
kill them

AISLADO

Abuelo holds the end of a broom halfway bent
over the pila, tries to scrub clean places in the walls
he can no longer reach. I climb into the water basin;
in the pila's dark corners hides an algae-eating fish.
I must catch it. With a bucket I make waves
in shallow water, search for what is tucked away from sight.
Abuelo says, *Me siento solo.* His days lonely, long
like the movie marathons he watches on TV.
The fish circles in a bowl. Already I know I won't visit
again tomorrow—know I don't love him anymore—
the magic of childhood gone like his clamorous
laugh, murky like the chaparro he still drinks. Abuelo
stares at the faucet. He tells me to guard the fish,
says if it hears water running from the tap it will jump.
Abuelo's eyes move slowly across the empty house, & we both
see the fish: its gills exposed on the empty basin's
concrete floor. Its fins shudder in air.

A MORNING EN LA CASA DE MI ABUELO

My mother cleans her father's toilet.
In her hand she holds a stale brush,
scrubs the concrete floor
of his washroom. Tomorrow
he'll tell her she will not inherit
this house or the land around it.
Tomorrow it will be her birthday;
he'll say he has to think
of his sons before his daughters—
an afterthought, like Abuela,
who always waited for his return—
palms open-faced & empty.
Today, my mother calls back to him,
¡Ayyy! Usted haga lo que le de la gana.
She washes her hands
before making dinner,
the skin on her fingers
still damp, still clinging.

TO WRITE MY MOTHER'S GOODBYE & FAIL

you're standing outside Abuela's house
staring into the dark empty doorway
saying goodbye to your brothers
you wear your nicest dress
white frill & nylons

you know this could be
goodbye forever (you are only eighteen & you paid
the coyote with borrowed money
from your oldest brother in Los Angeles)

you're standing in Buena Vista
& the desert already knows your name
you can hear it quietly calling you

your mother begs you
   not to leave

she says *chiquilla no te me vayas*
& no matter how sad she is
she refuses to cry
she won't even come outside
on the last day

you will still leave

        polvo rises behind you like the pale green walls
        of your mother's house
            you know from this moment on
        it will only exist in the mind
            in the in-between of your body

later when you cross a river with no name in Tijuana
hypothermia overtakes you
& you'll hear your mother quietly coo the hens
& the trees will billow over your heads

MAMÁ SAYS, *TODO LO QUE SE VE AQUÍ ES DESIERTO*

the desert vast unfolding
like skin across the landscape
of our lives
  is the only thing
  that exists here

at night we
breathe in stars
pull them from the sky
anchor ourselves
to things of the universe

there are no human forms here
the desert is the place
where we'll lose
all our humanity

or that is what they'll say of us

  how wild,
  how animal of them
  to think they could
  cross here

CALL ME REFUGEE VII

Llegamos al mirador
de la Puerta del Diablo*
donde todo el mundo es verde.
We climb up,
& below us carnival rides spin.

The screams of children are heard—
sus ecos cayéndose al fondo.
At the pinnacle
people take family photos;

they lean onto a single frayed rope
that signals:
aquí puedes caer a tu muerte.

El viento sacude la pita,
the only barrier between here
& where we should not pass.

but you know the truth:
  aquí es donde asesinaron a los secuestrados,
  los tiraban de este abismo.

The name of this place reminds you:
El diablo siempre estuvo aquí.

Remnants of the dead
fester beneath
layers of earth.
       & you imagine:
a captive's clasped hands,
their hooded heads unveiled
at the threshold of this ridge;
listen closely, oye bien el ruido
de sus cuerpos arrastrándose
todavía buscando al cielo.

  * In 1982, clandestine cemeteries were found at the Puerta del Diablo, San Salvador, and El Playón, La Libertad.

JONS MARKET ON 8TH & MARIPOSA

A journey through the desert brought you here. At eighteen you were living in the middle of Los Angeles a sea of people swarming past you: a young immigrant girl. You were determined to leave behind el cantón—your father drunk yelling into the open kitchen, your polio too. You wanted to forget, to not know the faces of the men who followed you home on those wet dirt roads.

You wandered these streets the same ones I roam now. I imagine you got lost, buildings melted into one another & streets unfolded into mazes. You were homesick. Everything was different yet somehow your neighbors were much like you: migrants to this city who cried only in Spanish. On a day when all you could do was hold back tears trying to translate labels in the aisles of a grocery store you saw the shadow of a body you knew like the smell of el río Las Minas. My father's large moustache could not hide that he was the same boy who teased you during school recess, the same boy whom you watched walk past your childhood home thousands of times. I wonder if he'd ever crossed your mind after he left for los Estados when you were thirteen, if you thought, *At some point we will meet again.*

You felt a rush of energy you could smell the wet dirt of el cantón. This is how I imagine you saw him; you must have wanted to hug. My father was also like you in this strange place. This unbelievable thing was a wave crashing over you unexpectedly & you emerged laughing your jaw wide open with joy & disbelief at finding yourselves en el otro lado. Everything you understood about "America" now felt like a small cantón & those aisles became dirt roads & you were children again passing each other on the way to somewhere.

If anyone said you'd find him in another country you would have thought them a fool. You said you didn't want a village boy. & yet the two of you were frozen in an alternate universe where the impossible was possible because you found the only other person in this faraway planet who knew the wet color of home.

WHITE MEMORIAL MEDICAL CENTER, BOYLE HEIGHTS, 1984

A hospital hallway is where I was nearly born. My mother waited for someone to gather me, but I crowned—una cabecita lista para el mundo—before anyone would believe a twenty-two-year-old girl.

My birth was full of toxic whiteness. Doctors clenched their white teeth. Nurses pressed their white mouths tight. They weren't concerned when my mother leaned into a waiting room chair, her pelvis forward, my head emerging. *¡Ya viene mi bebé! ¡Mi bebé!*

No one came for us. No one could hear a girl with broken English. The dome, the cathedral of my body, was emerging. & finally, when they were able to see I was really here, there was a sudden flood of bodies, & for a moment we were no longer invisible.

My father remained in the halls, searching for where we'd been taken. He thought he'd lost us. He asked, but no one listened. I imagine he paced up & down corridors, looking in the windows of all the locked doors until he found us. They never unbolted those doors. He watched my birth from a small window, as if it was not his to have.

The white doctors reminded us that we didn't belong here. When my father was finally able to see us, I smiled, & in that moment he was no longer invisible.

Now I stand outside. I stare at the place of my birth amid the buzzing of taco trucks, & if I listen closely I can hear babies being born in rooms flickering with uncertainty.

WHEN PEOPLE SAY: *BUT YOU WEREN'T BORN IN EL SALVADOR*

all the blood inside my body
is a stream tethered to the roots of trees
stretching thousands of years
they have carried me for generations
from the past into my physical body (the future)

i was always meant to be Guardado Guardado
my ancestral spirits guiando
mis padres (todavía solteros)
to the aisles of a grocery store
(a portal) to a cantón in Chalate

the damp marrow of my bones is filled
with the scent of el río Las Minas
where my great-great-grandmothers
gave birth to our bloodline
(nuestro mundo)
& quietly sang us into existence

Buena Vista is my destiny
i have no alternate origin story
my soul bloomed in the dark of Abuela's house
& migrated to another country
where my ancestors prayed for my parents
prayed over my unborn body
until my DNA was full of thunderstorms
until the day of my return
where my father (under pouring rain)
carried me across el río Las Minas
like baptism wading in water

MI QUERIDO EL SALVADOR,

Everyone says I should be afraid of you
as if you have never held me in your hands.
You have offered me what I cannot find anywhere else—
the way rain falls on tin roofs & mud sticks to our feet.
I know you've held my mother close
even though on most days she doesn't care to remember.
You haven't always been tender;
perhaps this is what you wanted to teach us:
that we too are here to die. Everyone says
I should be afraid of you, & sometimes I am—
at 3:30 a.m. when the dogs howl & howl.
We don't speak of the devil that invaded your home
even if we all know los Estados
killed your children, possessed your people,
raped & murdered what you love.
We refuse to see that the devil
still lives here. You've become a place
no one wants to understand.
But I want todos nosotros
to climb volcanoes full of fire,
to touch volcanic rock & black sand—
to look inside your heart.
Everyone says I should be afraid of you,
but all I want to do is return to you—
to run my hands through the humidity,
to let the fireflies call me tenderly into night,
to let you kiss me with the ashes on your tongue.

ABOUT THE AUTHOR

Cynthia Guardado is a Salvadorian American poet from Inglewood, California, and professor of English at Fullerton College. She is the managing editor of *LiveWire: A Literary Arts Journal.* She received her MFA from California State University, Fresno, and her debut poetry collection, *ENDEAVOR*, was published in 2017 by World Stage Press. Her work has appeared in *Poetry Magazine, Huizache, The Acentos Review, bozalta,* and *Wandering Song: Central American Writing in the United States.* Her book *Cenizas* was the winner of the 2016 Concurso Binacional de Poesía Pellicer-Frost (University of Texas at El Paso/S-Mart) and a finalist for the 2019 National Poetry Series Open Competition.